ISBN: 978-1-940087-47-4
21 Crows Dusk to Dawn Publishing, 21 Crows, LLC

I0113811

Monsters in the Hocking Hills

Table of Contents

Monsters in the Hocking Hills

Ash Cave to Cedar Falls
*State Route 56, South
Bloomingville, Ohio 43152
Parking at Ash Cave:
39.396088, -82.545740*
Hike from Ash Cave to Cedar Falls and back.
One way—2.5 miles.

Hunting the Hunters

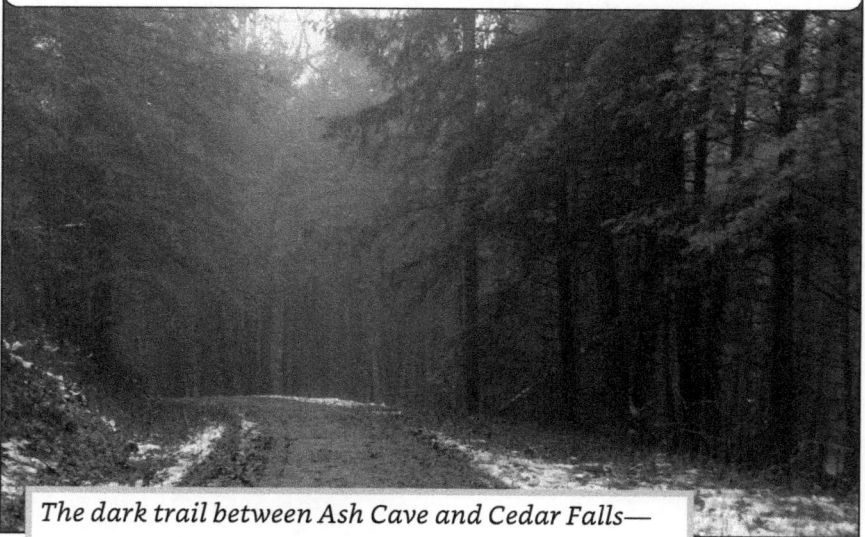

The dark trail between Ash Cave and Cedar Falls—

Hocking Hills State Park is visited by over five million tourists a year. They seek out the unique terrain—the recess caves, the cliffs, and the deep pockets of old forest. Sometimes, they find more than they expected. There have been Bigfoot sightings between Logan and Old Man's Cave and many reports of knocking and banging by campers at both private and state park campgrounds.

Along the popular park trails, it may not be easy to differentiate between the noises that hikers make and the sounds of a foraging creature. Still, the area is extensive with forests, natural areas, and national forests. Most parts of Hocking and nearby Vinton County are not heavily trafficked by humans—especially outside of summer and fall. Hocking Hills State Park is also strict about hikers staying directly on the trails—it is against the law to go off-trail because of the dangerous cliffs. When the parks close at dusk, the silence is deafening.

No trails seem to compete better for Bigfoot sightings than the region between Ash Cave and Rose Lake. A hilly path leads through the Hocking State Forest located between the two with hemlocks and massive beech trees. Along the way, there are meandering creeks and old logging roads. It was one of these very paths hunters were using when one had a very startling experience with a Bigfoot!

The trail can be busy in the summer, but in late autumn and winter, it can be a lonely walk where you may be more apt to find evidence of Bigfoot.

Four men were hunting in a designated hunting area in autumn in the forestry area between Cedar Falls and Ash Cave. They broke off into a couple of different parties. While one group worked their way along a trail, one man began to smell something putrid like rotting meat. Scoffing if off as nothing more than decaying vegetation, they continued onward. Along the way, they noticed a bare footprint, which was decidedly strange for October.

In the afternoon, there was rustling in the brush. One of the men decided to check it out, descending the hill before he stopped. To his surprise, he saw something he could not quite fathom even for an experienced hunter—a seven-foot-tall ape-like creature covered with dark brown hair and having a human-like nose, thick brow ridges, and a sloped forehead. He hastily returned and said it was time to leave. Returning on following hunting seasons, he would have additional sightings, find footprints, and even hear a growl.

**Rose Lake
Fisherman's Access**
**21114-20530 OH-374
Logan, Ohio 43138
Parking:
39.432044, -82.528346**

Face to Face With a Hairy Ape

Rose Lake is near the Hocking Hills State Park Campground. By day, it can be busy with hikers and folks fishing. But when evening rolls in, it is pretty quiet. The perfect time, perhaps, for fishing and sighting a Bigfoot too.

Rose Lake: *You can access Rose Lake with a 1/2 mile hike from the parking lot off Route 374: (39.432044, -82.528346)*

At Rose Lake, a father and son came face to face with a hairy, ape-like creature while walking the trail around the lake. The father reported the event to park officers, who scanned the area but found no trace of the creature.

Rockbridge State Nature Preserve
11460 Dalton Road
Rockbridge, Ohio 43149
Parking:
39.567122, -82.499324
(no pets)
1.75 mile loop trail

Incident at the Rock Bridge

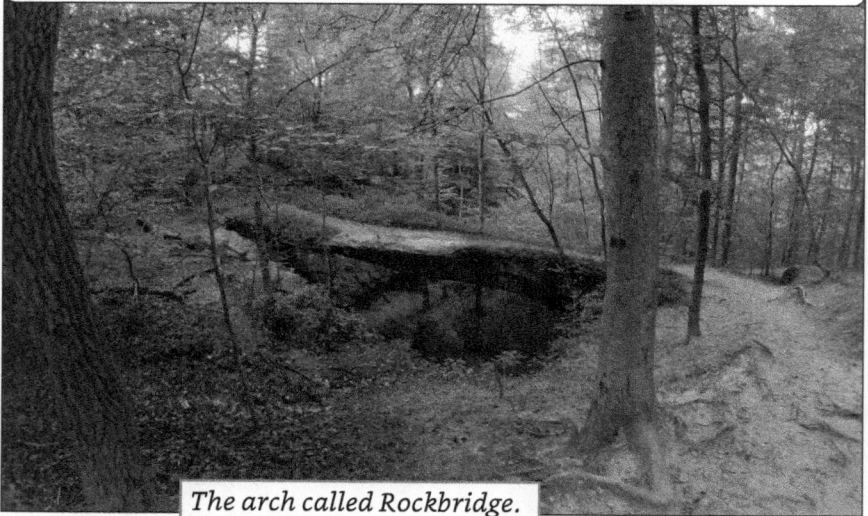

The arch called Rockbridge.

In a state nature preserve between Lancaster and Logan, there is a large natural stone arch called Rockbridge above a deep ravine. The surrounding area is sparsely populated with pockets of farmland and forest, not far from the Hocking River. However, tourists visit here often, taking in the unique arch. Occasionally, these day trippers come across strange sights and sounds as they walk. One later afternoon in June of 2017, a man taking the hike crossed the rock bridge and continued on the path back to his vehicle.

Around one twist in the trail, he heard the crash of something large running through the woods and cutting through the brush and trees. Thinking he had spooked a deer, he continued onward. Then, at one bend, he discovered a large footprint deeply embedded in the dirt path. When he quickly snatched up his camera and took a couple of shots, whatever had run in the woods appeared to be still around as above his head, and in the tree canopy, something made a horrible crashing sound. It was enough to send the man at a more hurried pace to his vehicle.

Later, investigators Bea Mills and Marc DeWerth of the Bigfoot Field Researchers Organization returned to research the man's report given to them, and the footprints were still there! They measured nearly 18.5 inches in length.

Twists and turns along the path—Rockbridge State Nature Preserve is between Lancaster and Logan. The trail can be accessed by the parking lot. Some may believe that this area is too close to civilization to have much Bigfoot activity. I am not so sure. The habitat is diverse with areas of thicker forest, fenced cattle pasture where tourists cannot enter, and brush offering both places to hide and a varied source of food.

**Clear Creek Metro Park
Benua Lake Trail**
195 Clear Creek Road
Rockbridge, Ohio 43149
39.594120, -82.621947
Parking at Fishing Access #8
Behind park office

Clear Creek Creature

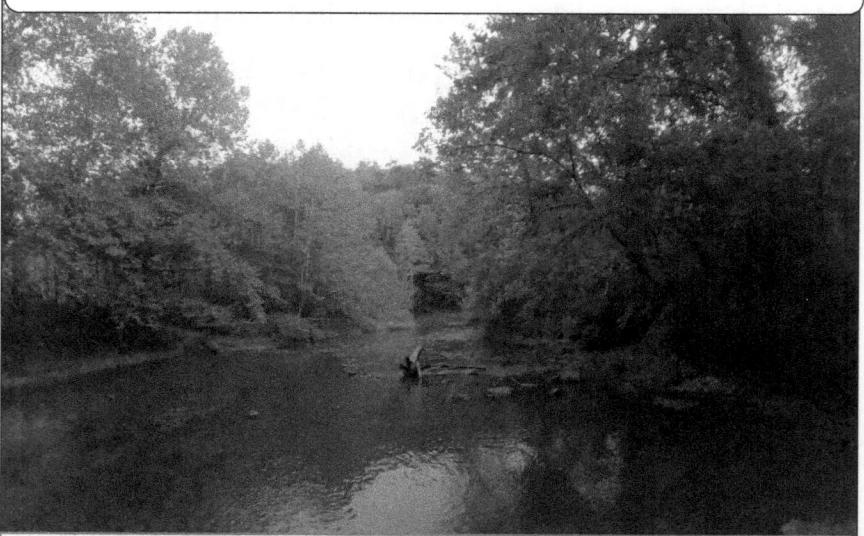

Along the Benua Lake Trail, the closest public trail in the park to Snortin Ridge and a great place to explore for signs of Bigfoot.

Snortin Ridge Road runs just outside the boundaries of Clear Creek Metro Park and is close to the town of Revenge. Locals have heard mysterious screams, mumblings, and growls within this area abutting the park not far from Benua Lake. Additionally, they have witnessed a hulking creature walking near their properties.

On a chilly night with rain on the horizon, a group of teens set off on family property to try to get a picture of the creature making the noises. Several broke away from the group and marched on ahead, intending to jump out to startle the rest when they caught up. As they settled into the woods, crouching and awaiting the remainder of the teens, they heard a noise near an abandoned and tumbledown cabin nearby. One shined a flashlight towards the noise and, basked beyond the light, was the silhouette of a huge creature! They all turned and fled at that moment and did not stop along the quarter-mile run back to the house.

Trails are well-maintained, but just off the beaten path, there are plenty of places for wildlife to secret themselves.
When I was searching for places to find the elusive creature in the Hocking Hills, the first person I went to was Bea Mills. Not only is she an authority on Bigfoot, but she is the Ohio investigator for Bigfoot Field Researchers Organization. She offered up the information on the Snortin Ridge and Clear Creek area. So it is certainly one huge area you want to check out!

Clear Creek Metro Park
Lake Ramona—Lake Trail
918 Co Hwy 69
Lancaster, Ohio 43130
Accesses: Valley View Picnic
Parking: 39.60019, -82.631693
Trailhead: 39.600281, -82.632913
Moderate 1.2 mile loop
leading to an observation deck
overlooking Lake Ramona

Photoshoot

Lake Trail leading to Lake Ramona just before dusk—

In the autumn of 2010, a professional photographer on a photoshoot along with two of his clients witnessed tree knocking, rock-throwing, and limb breaking at Lake Ramona in Clear Creek Metro Park. Curious, he took several photos of the area of the commotion. Upon returning home, he had several images of what appeared to be a black orangutan!

Vinton Furnace

Stone Quarry Road
McArthur, Ohio 45651
Parking:
39.213791, -82.397786
You can walk the old roads around the old furnace or follow Elk Fork.
Vinton Furnace
Experimental Station:
Parking:
39.191013, -82.405794

The Darkling of Vinton Furnace

Along an old road at Vinton Furnace.

Between August and October of 1980, there were a series of highly publicized reports of a Bigfoot in the area of McArthur, including footprints and sightings. A monster-mania pursued, and as the years passed, the stories became so popular that in May of 1988, a camo-clad and heavily armed party of hunters descended into McArthur's hills and valleys and set up something similar to a military encampment to track this monster down.

Troops divided into two teams run as an armed posse and trailed by newspaper reporters and photographers marched off to the beat of a dismal cool rain to search from dusk to dawn. They came back to the encampment empty-handed, and later some researchers suggested that the later tales were a hoax.

But some were not. For over 80 years, stories have popped up around the communities of McArthur, Prattsville, and now towns long-gone about a large, dark creature seen along the isolated wilderness area around Elk Fork and the vicinity of Vinton Furnace. Most describe it as Bigfoot-like, curious, and elusive. For example, Hamden local Mike Claar spotted a Bigfoot near McArthur in the 1980s and stated, "It looked a lot like an ape," he told reporters. "The darned thing was at least 10 feet tall, and it had real long arms. The odor it gave off was just awful. It was pungent . . . like maybe that creature hadn't had a bath in about a year." But even earlier, in the 1950s, a 5-6-year-old girl on a farm near Prattsville was playing in the yard when she noticed a Bigfoot close enough that she could nearly reach out and touch it. She panicked, ran inside, and hid behind the couch. And she kept it secret from even her family. It was not until many years later that she divulged the traumatic experience to her brother.

Over the years, when I tell locals that one of my favorite hiking places are the many trails of the remote Vinton Furnace and the surrounding forestry area, I have had a few who offer up a questioning furrow of the brow. "You go out there?" they ask. I bob my head up and down. Then they tell me that they do not believe in Bigfoot or ghosts, but just in case, I should watch out. Because they or someone in their family saw something big, dark, and strange in those woods while they were hunting or hanging out there. I wait for them to laugh. They do not. And so I do watch out.

Vinton Furnace to McArthur
Stone Quarry Road and State Route 50
McArthur, Ohio 45651
Parking:
39.213791, -82.397786

Wild Cat

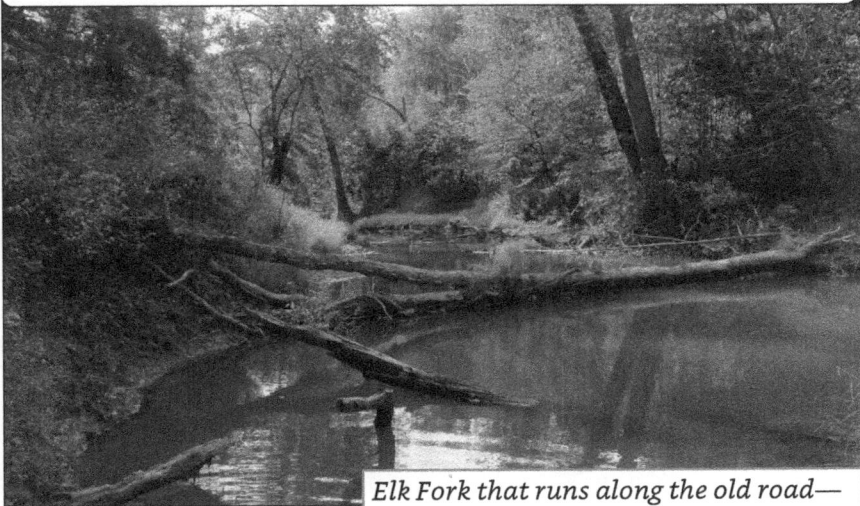

Elk Fork that runs along the old road—

Legends have always circulated around the Vinton Furnace Experimental Station and the outlying Vinton Forest that a large cougar-like cat prowls. No one has established if it was someone's pet mountain lion who was cute as a kitten, but got too big to handle and was released. Or if it is the legendary Wampus Cat, half-human and half-cat from Appalachian folklore—a witch who was caught in mid-spell turning herself into a cat and remains for eternity trapped between the two.

When I moved to the county many years ago, our real estate agent told us she and another agent assessed some property between Prattsville and McArthur. The two had to slog back through the brush probably a quarter-mile on an overgrown drive. It was a difficult task as both were wearing business attire, including a cotton skirt, blouse, and high heels. The trek to the property was a slow process as they had to veer around the briars that begged to catch on their clothing, and their heels jabbed deep into the dirt.

About thirty minutes passed before they finally made it to the lot, evaluated the grounds, and shot some pictures. As they turned to leave, my realtor noticed something moving out of the corner of her eyes. She blinked, narrowed her gaze, then took in the form of a large mountain lion gazing in their direction, keeling slightly forward and ever-so-slightly wiggling its butt.

She proceeded to tell me that its long tail was swishing back and forth, and I interrupted her because I imagined my old fat tomcat using those same movements. It always meant that he was getting ready to pounce on my moving feet as if my toes were easy prey. "Holy crap, what did you do?" I asked with bated breath. "I think it was readying to eat you. You were a half-hour from your truck!"

And she replied quite unassumingly, "Not on the way back, we weren't!"

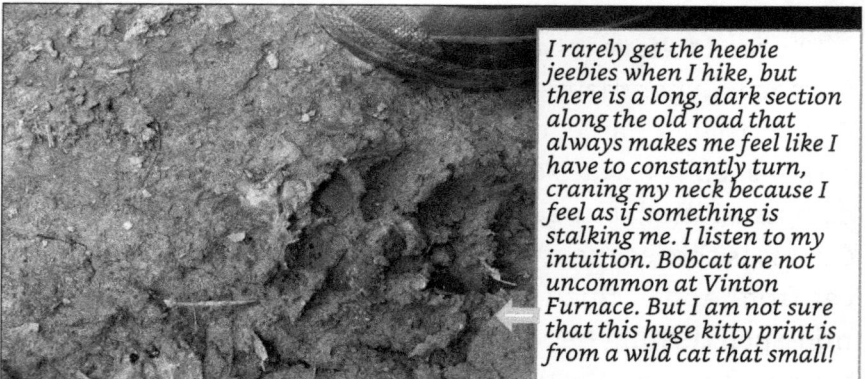

I rarely get the heebie jeebies when I hike, but there is a long, dark section along the old road that always makes me feel like I have to constantly turn, craning my neck because I feel as if something is stalking me. I listen to my intuition. Bobcat are not uncommon at Vinton Furnace. But I am not sure that this huge kitty print is from a wild cat that small!

Ghosts in the Hocking Hills

Table of Contents

Ghosts in the Hocking Hills

Old Man's Cave
Hocking Hills State Park
OH-664
Logan, Ohio 43138
39.438049, -82.537987

The Legend of Old Man's Cave and the Baying Hound

OLD MAN'S CAVE

Old Man's Cave in earlier times.

There once was a quiet town between Logan and South Bloomingville called Cedar Grove. It was settled near a sandstone gorge with a meandering stream called Cedar Creek that ran beneath the cliffs. Many years ago, two young boys who lived in the town were exploring the valley and its many nooks and crannies. Growing bored after climbing one boulder after another, they built a small fire within a large recess cave that overlooked a valley of hemlocks and craggy rocks.

One of the boys, the younger of the two, was uncertain about visiting this particular cave. It was rumored to be haunted. Some had heard the low baying of a hound at night there, but when they searched for the dog, it could never be found. The boys had only been inside the cave a few minutes when the crunch of footsteps on leaves and sand forced them to look up from the flames. An old man and a large, white dog, staying close to the man's side, walked past them. The man had a long, gray beard, old-fashioned clothing, and leather moccasins. He carried an antique rifle over his shoulder. The man appeared to be interested in the back of the cave. He paced back and forth near the edge of the far rocks and, upon coming to a standstill, peered intently at a shallow depression in the sandstone earth. Then both the man and the dog vanished into the depression as if they had not been there at all!

Eagerly, the boys sought help from some local adults at Cedar Grove, investigating the place the old man had disappeared. With mattocks and shovels, a small crew of men removed rocks and dug out the hollow in the cave's sandstone floor. They exposed two sets of bones—a man and a dog, an old flintlock rifle with the date of 1702 etched into the wood, and some cooking pots. There was also a scratching in the stone that stated the man's name and the date of his death as 1777. For quite some time, many travelers would come to visit to see the remains inside the cave they dubbed Dead Man's Cave or Old Man's Cave. They would stare down at them and wonder who the man and dog had once been. Some would hear the baying of a hound dog far away, and rumors prevailed that the ghostly dog returned, but for what reason, they did not know. After a while, the bones disappeared. The curious stopped coming, and the story faded away except for a few living in the community, who brought it up once in a while when lingering outside the grocery store.

Old Man's Cave today.

One late autumn night not too long ago, a park ranger listened intently to the sound of a dog howling deep in the gorge. Occasionally, dogs from the scattering of homes nearby strayed from their backyards. They usually found their way home, but this particular dog sounded like a hunting hound, and the frantic bay most certainly meant it had treed a raccoon. It could mean that poachers were hunting in the park.

The ranger snatched up his flashlight and worked his way down the rugged trail and into the gorge. He followed the sound of the dog, filtering out the splash of a waterfall and the crunch of sandstone at his feet. But even while he got closer to the hound's yowling howls and threw the beam of his flashlight upward, he could see little in the fog flowing up along the rock cliff. He saw no dog in the darkness. And yet, the howls got louder and louder until they seemed to be circling him just out of reach. He whipped his flashlight around in a circle, then just as suddenly as the dog's baying came, it ceased.

For years, many have heard the baying of a phantom dog within the gorge and cave area called Old Man's Cave. Its presence is explained like this—

Before the settling of the towns of Logan and Cedar Grove, some trappers lived along Cedar Creek, a stream that worked its way through a deep sandstone gorge. These men made their home in modest one-room cabins or animal-skin tents abutting the small caves within the valley. They made a living selling the pelts of the many fur-bearing creatures like otter and fox that roamed the region at the time.

As their jobs required them to travel far into the wilderness, they were gone for many days at a time. One winter, upon returning from a seasonal hunt, neighbors noticed that one particular trapper named Retzler, who made his home in a cave outcropping along with his dog Harper had not been seen in quite some time. The usually heavily-traveled path to his abode was overgrown, and there was no sign of his faithful hound who bayed whenever someone neared the camp.

After taking the footpath that led to the cave, they lifted the flap of his leather-hide tent and peered inside. Before them lay the dead trapper along with his old hound dog dead by his side. They carefully lifted the limp bodies of the man and dog and placed them in a shallow hole they had dug in the back of the cave and covered them with sand.

Ash Cave
Hocking Hills State Park
27292 OH-56
South Bloomingville, Ohio 43152
39.395993, -82.545927

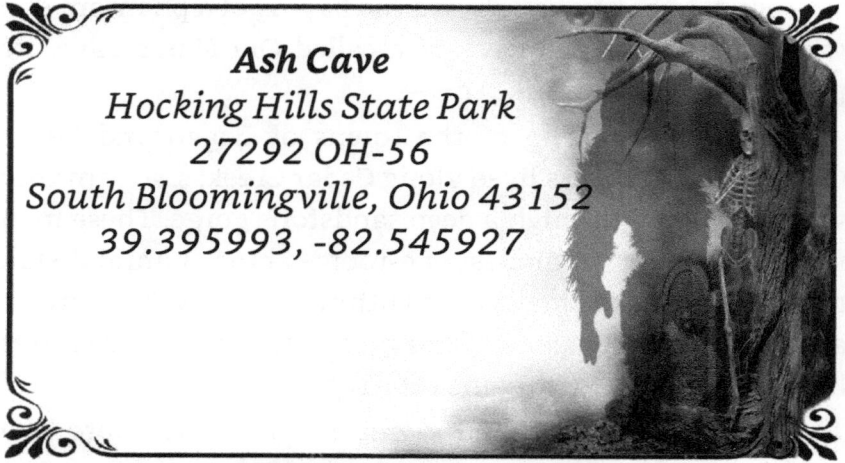

Vanishing Hiker of Ash Cave

Ash Cave, named for the large amount of ashes early settlers found piled high on the sand floor of the recess cave and considered to be the remnants of Indian campfires.

Early one spring, Pat Quackenbush, park naturalist, led hikers on a special night tour. It was a short hike along a concrete walkway a half-mile to one particularly large recess in the sandstone called Ash Cave, where a waterfall cascades down a cliff.

It was a small group of twelve people, and this night as they walked, he would pause beneath the hemlocks and cliffs and face the group, pointing out unique features along the route. Each time they stopped, he would make a quick headcount silently to himself to make sure everyone kept up with him. He did not want anyone lost in the dark! "—*ten, eleven, twelve*—" Once Pat could see he had accounted for everyone, he called attention to a deer almost hidden and grazing in the grass. He then piped up with a barred owl's call that, almost immediately, was returned with a couple of hoots from deep in the forest.

He always paused before each stop; there were usually one or two stragglers in the line who would get caught up in the charm of the fairyland-like trail. "—*ten, eleven,*" he counted in his head. "*Yep—twelve. All there.*" And, if needed, Pat would patiently wait for a minute or two, so anyone left behind could catch up before he doled out another trinket or two about the unique area around them.

The trail leading to Ash Cave.

About a quarter of the way, he realized that one dawdler had seemed to creep from the shadows right before he started his spiel. "—*ten, eleven, twelve—and,*" he counted. "*Hmmm, thirteen?*" At first, Pat thought perhaps he had counted the number of people wrong when they met. Maybe this extra hiker had been enjoying the walk alone under the huge hemlocks and wanted some time away from the rest of the group. It was not as troubling that there was one *more* person added to the group than there was one *less.* So instead of waiting and making a recount, the naturalist decided to continue, knowing the straggler would eventually catch up with the group.

Pat along the trail with a group near the spot that a peculiar hiker has been known to join the group.

He was about halfway to the cave when he stopped long enough to talk about an ancient beech tree near the trail. The group had made a half-circle around him, and while they did, he made a great effort to count everyone quickly. "—*ten, eleven, twelve——*" He glanced up and noticed the straggler was only about five feet from the hikers. "*Thirteen!*" He had counted correctly!

But number thirteen was not like the rest. He noted she was wearing old-fashioned clothing—a feed sack dress commonly worn by the thrifty women in the 19th-century depression era who used flour and feed sacks to make their clothing. The mysterious guest was so out-of-place with the group, he was thrown off-guard and simply brought it to everyone's attention. "I turned my attention behind the group," Pat said, "and proceeded to ask if they could see the woman who was standing there and had been following us. I watched them reluctantly turn, and there were more than a few gasps. I wasn't alone. Everyone on that hike saw her." Then she took two steps and disappeared into the woods.

Since then, others have brought the lone hiker that strays behind the group to his attention. Once in a while, witnesses have reported seeing a woman peeking from behind a tree. Then she vanishes from sight.

There is quite a lot of speculation of the identity of the ghostly lady at Ash Cave. Some believe it is a woman who lived in a house across the road who visited the cave often and now returns in ghostly form to walk the area she loved. But no one knows who it is for sure. The cave's shelter has been used by traveling Indians, early settlers as a home, and local preachers once held camp meetings at the cave, as above. The cave provided great acoustics, especially from one large stone where preachers stood which was dubbed Pulpit Rock.

Cedar Falls
Hocking Hills State Park
OH-374
Logan, Ohio 43138
39.419485, -82.524121
Parking: 39.417131, -82.525612

The Road to Hell

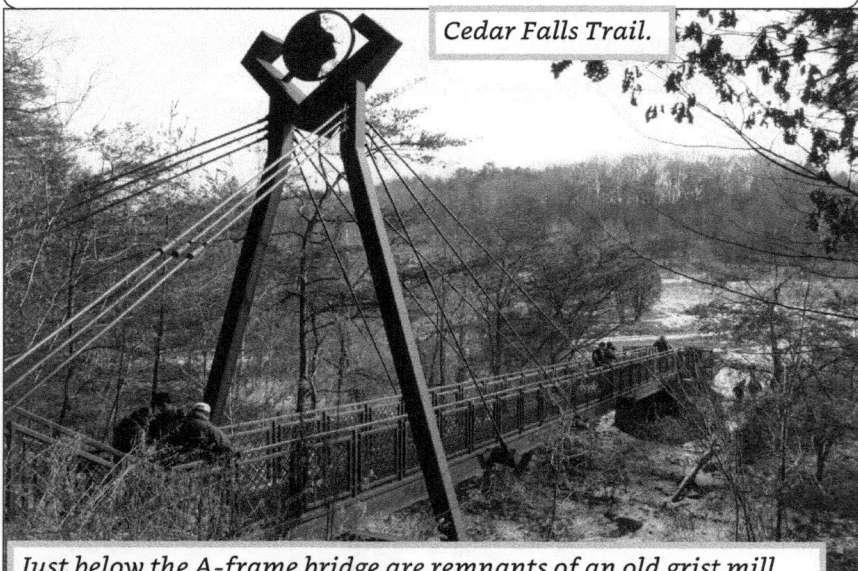

Cedar Falls Trail.

Just below the A-frame bridge are remnants of an old grist mill once powered by the flowing waters of Queer Creek. Queer Creek was so named because until it joins with Cedar Creek, it flows in a backward, northerly direction. Creeks in southern Ohio typically flow in a southerly direction.

In the early 1800s, a grist-mill powered by the waters of Queer Creek, sat on the rim of Cedar Falls. Nearby was a massive beech tree with words engraved deeply in its ancient trunk, "This is the road to hell, 1782."

The tree was along a dark, tree-covered trail that worked its way deep into the gorge. It was often used by Indians traveling to Chillicothe around the time tempers were high between settlers and Indians. It was speculated often by those visiting the mill in days long past that settlers had been marched along this rugged path strewn with boulders and murdered along the route after one particular raid. One such trapper was captured by the Indians and camped beneath its wide canopy one night. As the story goes, his beard was pulled from the roots and he was burned and branded with pine knots, an especially hot piece of wood. After suffering untold agony, he was able to escape into the wilderness and towards what is now Ash Cave, but not before etching those words into the tree. On moonless nights, the screams of others who did not escape are heard issuing from the valley where the mill once stood, not far from the bridge along the Cedar Falls trail.

Queer Creek just below the area of the mill and the view from the bridge. The beech tree is no longer standing, but the area where it stood is not far from the Cedar Falls trail: Trailhead Parking (39.418280, -82.526489)

Rock House
Hocking Hills State Park
16350 OH-374
Laurelville, Ohio 43135
39.495457, -82.615055

In the Garden

Rock House.

There is a sandstone cave with a tunnel-like passage at Hocking Hills State Park. It is best known as Rock House. Within, those with a keen eye can find small squares dug into the earth that were troughs dug by early inhabitants of the area to catch water for drinking. Old-timers have long passed down legends that robbers once used the cavern as a hideout, and it earned the nickname Robbers Roost.

Afterward, many curious travelers came from faraway to peer into its depths and wonder what villainous deeds those outlaws had accomplished.

Sometime after the Civil War, a 16-room summer resort stood at the top of Rock House near the present-day shelter house. It offered luxury accommodations, pretty gardens, and a view of the cave within a short walking distance. Then, people traveled once again to see the forest and rock formations far away from the towns and cities.

Rock House Hotel and the garden in earlier years where a ghost would make an appearance. And perhaps still does!

After many years, the hotel went out of business, the building fell into ruins, and nobody visited there anymore except to see the cave. It was around this time that the place where the old hotel had stood was rumored to be haunted. Passersby would see a ghostly woman walk from where the hotel's door used to be and make her way to the gardens, now overgrown with vines, brush, and briers. She lingered there for a short time, then faded away.

**Conkles Hollow State
Nature Preserve
Hocking Hills State Park**
*24132 Big Pine Road
Rockbridge, Ohio 43149
39.453492, -82.572727*

Haunted Hollow

The haunted hollow.

Just a little off Big Pine Road in an area that has never been more than sparsely habited, there is a dark hollow. Few people have ever lived there long because of the strange happenings within. Deep moans issue from the bowels of the valley, and on certain nights, screams are heard there. Three men were murdered here, and it is their voices carried with the wind. Their story has been passed on as this—

During the mid-1700s, flatboats carried families along the Ohio River and the many smaller rivers, searching for a place to settle. There were many fights between the settlers and Shawnee, Wyandot, and Delaware over the land, and attacks on travelers were common. One such group of warriors set out one day to rob flatboats as they came through a narrow, shallow pass along the Ohio River. Once they raided the passengers, they would flee into the unsettled areas of the wilderness that is now the Hocking Hills, pausing long enough to secret their stash in the many small caves of the region.

After several such raids, word traveled about the dangerous and shallow pass where Indians ambushed boats. Some voyagers tried to avoid the pass along the river altogether, while others had no choice, with the large number of possessions they carried, to take the chance they might be bushwhacked. One expedition was especially fearful of taking the route. They had brought with them all they owned within the boat and among their possessions was a chest filled with many silver coins.

The fearful settlers developed a plan to elude the Indians at this point on their journey. They sent one flatboat ahead with the women, children, and their goods. Just behind would be a posse of men, horses, and guns in a second boat laying in wait and ready to stop the thieves.

On this particular trip, a band of only three Indians hijacked the boat. As the warriors seized upon their treasures and opened the chest filled with coins, they delighted in their good luck, but they failed to question why there were no men among the boat passengers until it was too late. Unexpectedly, the second flatboat with the men and weapons rounded the bend in the river and came upon the thieves.

The posse landed their boat, jumped to their horses, and grabbed their guns to give a chase. They pursued the three warriors relentlessly for days. At some point, the three Indians, believing they had outrun the posse, slowed as they came into a dark valley between two high hills with a small stream running between them. They rested there a day, stuffing their loot into the nooks and crannies of the sandstone cliff walls, handfuls of coins thrust within and all the way back to the end of the narrow creek valley where they could go no farther as it ended in a sheer cliff wall. There they stopped and readied to leave. But not before the thieves heard the sound of horses huffing in the cool, damp air. One Indian looked back and, realizing they had trapped themselves within the hollow, prepared to fight, but the settlers outnumbered them. There was no escape, and the posse murdered the men within the hollow.

The end of the line for the thieves. There was no way out.

The settlers found some of the stolen goods, but no one ever recovered the many silver coins. Even though a thorough search was made within the hollow, their whereabouts were a mystery. The place almost immediately became a terrifying area to visit after dark. Moans and groans swept out from the hollow, and ghosts played pranks on those walking within as if they wanted to keep them out.

According to one of the volunteers who helps with the state park activities, strange things do occur within the hollow. She was setting up Tiki bamboo torches along the trail with several young volunteers so visitors could see the path during a night hike at Conkles Hollow. It was a new moon night and very dark. The crew had yet to light the torches, waiting until it was completely dark outside. The four dawdled at a small cave in the bend of the trail and readied with rechargeable lighters and matches to fire up the torch wicks—"When we felt it was dark enough, we all picked a torch to light but as hard as we tried, we could not get any of them to light," she divulged. "Every time we lit a match, it was like a puff of someone's breath blowing it out.

Every time we flicked the lighter, it simply would not give us a flame. We had to stagger blindly all the way back to the parking lot in the pitch-black for more matches. All the while, it was deathly quiet around us except a low, hushed whisper we prayed was the creek. Not even the sound of crickets or a deer bumbling around in the leaves in the dark came to our ears. We returned, and suddenly, the old lighters seemed to work and the crickets and birds started chirping again."

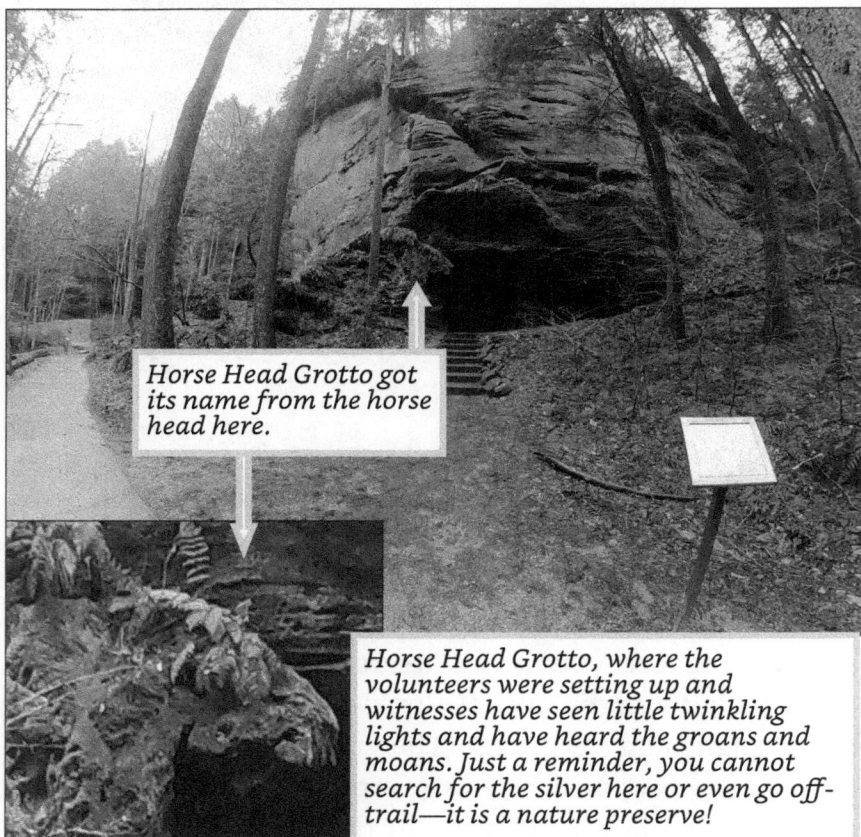

Horse Head Grotto got its name from the horse head here.

Horse Head Grotto, where the volunteers were setting up and witnesses have seen little twinkling lights and have heard the groans and moans. Just a reminder, you cannot search for the silver here or even go off-trail—it is a nature preserve!

Citations

Hocking:
-The Hocking Sentinel. June 22, 1905. The Wonderland of Hocking Dead Man's Cave
-Logan Hocking Sentinel July 21, 1853
-The Democrat-sentinel., August 12, 1909
-The Democrat-sentinel., August 15, 1907
-The Democrat-sentinel., February 25, 1909
-The Democrat-sentinel., March 28, 1907 Interesting Story of Old Man's Cave
-The Hocking sentinel., June 22, 1905
-Bea Mills. (n.d.). BFRO report 57774: Possible footprint find near Rockbridge state nature preserve. Retrieved from https://bfro.net/GDB/show_report.asp?id=57774
-BFRO report 3920: Hunters have several encounters near ash cave state Park. (n.d.). Retrieved from https://bfro.net/GDB/show_report.asp?id=3920
-BFRO report 8450: Property owners hear loud vocalizations in early morning and have a possible sighting near Clearcreek metro Park. (n.d.). Retrieved from https://www.bfro.net/GDB/show_report.asp?id=8450

Vinton:
-Athens Sunday Messenger March 11, 1923
-Republican Enquirer. (McArthur, Ohio) March 29, 1920. Vinton County. 114 Years Ago in Vinton County History, By Our Route 2 Correspondent.
-BFRO report 4982: Personal encounter of a camper as well as a history of encounters concerning his family members, dating back 40 years. (n.d.). Retrieved from https://www.bfro.net/GDB/show_report.asp?id=4982

www.ingramcontent.com/pod-product-compliance
Lightning Source LLC
Chambersburg PA
CBHW030000290326
41935CB00008B/643